the

every...an

being God's ma... in the ...ation

series

Real Men. Real Life. Powerful Truth.

Stephen Arterburn

Kenny Luck & Todd Wendorff

WATERBROOK
PRESS

BEING GOD'S MAN…IN THE FACE OF TEMPTATION
PUBLISHED BY WATERBROOK PRESS
2375 Telstar Drive, Suite 160
Colorado Springs, Colorado 80920
A division of Random House, Inc.

ISBN 1-57856-681-9

Published in association with the literary agency of Alive Communications, Inc., 7680 Goddard Street, Suite 200, Colorado Springs, CO 80920.

Printed in the United States of America
2005

10 9 8 7 6 5 4

contents

welcome to the every man
Bible study series

As Christian men, we crave true-to-life, honest, and revealing Bible study curricula that will equip us for the battles that rage in our lives. We are looking for resources that will get us into our Bibles in the context of mutually accountable relationships with other men. But like superheroes who wear masks and work hard to conceal their true identities, most of us find ourselves isolated and working alone on the major issues we face. Many of us present a carefully designed public self, while hiding our private self from view. This is not God's plan for us.

Let's face it. We all have trouble being honest with ourselves, particularly in front of other men.

As developers of a men's ministry, we believe that many of the problems among Christian men today are direct consequences of an inability to practice biblical openness—being honest about our struggles, questions, and temptations—and to connect with one another. Our external lives may be in order, but storms of unprocessed conflict, loss, and fear are eroding our resolve to maintain integrity. Sadly, hurting Christian men are flocking to unhealthy avenues of relief instead of turning to God's Word and to one another.

We believe the solution to this problem lies in creating opportunities for meaningful relationships among men. That's why we designed this Bible study series to be thoroughly interactive. When a man practices biblical openness with other men, he moves from secrecy to candor, from isolation to connection, and from pretense to authenticity.

Kenny and Todd developed the study sessions at Saddleback Church in Lake Forest, California, where they teach the men's morning Bible studies. There, men hear an outline of the Bible passage, read the verses together, and then answer a group discussion question at their small-group tables. The teaching pastor then facilitates further discussion within the larger group.

This approach is a huge success for many reasons, but the key is that, deep down, men really do want close friendships with other guys. We don't enjoy living on the barren islands of our own secret struggles. However, many men choose to process life, relationships, and pressures individually because they fear the vulnerability required in small-group gatherings. *Suppose someone sees behind my carefully constructed image? Suppose I encounter rejection after revealing one of my worst sins?* Men willingly take risks in business and the stock market, sports and recreation, but we do not easily risk our inner lives.

Many church ministries are now helping men win this battle, providing them with opportunities to experience Christian male companionship centered in God's Word. This study series aims to supplement and expand that good work around the country. If these lessons successfully reach you, then they will also reach every relationship and domain that you influence. That is our heartfelt prayer for every man in your group.

how to use this study guide

As you prepare for each session, first review the **Key Verse** and **Goals for Growth,** which reveal the focus of the study at hand. Discuss as a group whether or not you will commit to memorizing the Key Verse for each session. The **Head Start** section then explains why these goals are necessary and worthwhile. Each member of your small group should complete the **Connect with the Word** section *before* the small-group sessions. Consider this section to be your personal Bible study for the week. This will ensure that everyone has spent some time interacting with the biblical texts for that session and is prepared to share responses and personal applications. (You may want to mark or highlight any questions that were difficult or particularly meaningful, so you can focus on those during the group discussion.)

When you gather in your small group, you'll begin by reading aloud the **Head Start** section to remind everyone of the focus for the current session. The leader will then invite the group to share any questions, concerns, insights, or comments arising from their personal Bible study during the past week. If your group is large, consider breaking into subgroups of three or four people (no more than six) at this time.

Next get into **Connect with the Group,** starting with the **Group Opener.** These openers are designed to get at the heart of each week's lesson. They focus on how the men in your group relate to the passage and topic you are about to discuss. The group leader will read the opener for that week's session aloud and then facilitate interaction on the **Discussion Questions** that follow. (Remember: Not everyone has to offer an answer for every question.)

Leave time after your discussion to complete the **Standing Strong** exercises, which challenge each man to consider, *What's my next move?* As you openly express your thoughts to the group, you'll be able to hold one another accountable to reach for your goals.

Finally, close in **prayer,** either in your subgroups or in the larger group. You may want to use this time to reflect on and respond to what God has done in your group during the session. Also invite group members to share their personal joys and concerns, and use this as "grist" for your prayer time together.

By way of review, each lesson is divided into the following sections:

To be read or completed *before* the small-group session:
- **Key Verse**
- **Goals for Growth**
- **Head Start**
- **Connect with the Word** (home Bible study: 30-40 minutes)

To be completed *during* the small-group session:
- Read aloud the **Head Start** section (5 minutes)
- Discuss personal reaction to **Connect with the Word** (10 minutes)
- **Connect with the Group** (includes the **Group Opener** and discussion of the heart of the lesson: 30-40 minutes)
- **Standing Strong** (includes having one person pray for the group; challenges each man to take action: 20 minutes)

avoiding the serpent

Why study the topic of temptation? Because all men are tempted to compromise their spiritual and moral integrity by yielding to unhealthy passions and desires. And yet not all men do. Some have learned the secret of living an undivided life in which their thoughts and actions actually reflect their beliefs. How can we learn their secret? How can we face temptation without yielding? How can we avoid the Serpent's smooth and persuasive talk?

In our one-on-one work with men in the church, we have discovered the top eight temptations all men face.

Every man is tempted to

- fold when hard times come;
- have an undisciplined thought life;
- give in to sexual temptation;
- fudge when it comes to obedience;
- compare himself with and judge others;
- let loose with his tongue in anger;
- believe the myth of materialism; and
- live in isolation from other men.

We have also learned that dealing with these temptations is truly a matter of survival. We can't venture out into a field of land mines without taking precautions. Every man needs to know where the mines are and how to avoid them.

How we choose to respond in the midst of excruciating inner impulses will either leave us spiritually bankrupt or will move us a step closer to a Christlike heart and character. Character grows strong only as we exercise moral and spiritual integrity. This Bible study will help you do just that. We have selected the New Testament book of James for this study because it addresses, in a hard-hitting way, the top temptations men face. James writes to men. He speaks our language. He's direct and easy to understand. He calls us to action.

And life is all about action—making wise choices daily. In fact, life is a series of Will I...? questions. Will I give in to this temptation or not? Will I look? Will I cheat? Will I compromise? Will I lie? Will I presume? Will I...? As we learn to think clearly and choose wisely, our character becomes firmly established. And each time we choose to walk away from the Tempter, we strengthen the foundation of the godly life we are hoping to build over time, a life characterized by integrity.

Godly men have this solid foundation. They've gained new perspectives on the trials and temptations they face; they possess new tools that save them from impulsive responses; they exhibit new behaviors that produce a God-given humility and flexibility; and they know that confession breaks the power of temptation, and connection with other men sustains the victory.

Our goal in this study is to stimulate personal reflection and honest dialogue with God and with other men. As you work through each session, look in the mirror at your own life and ask yourself some hard questions. Whether you are doing this study individually or in a group, realize that being completely honest with yourself, with God, and with others will produce the greatest growth.

In the sessions that follow, you will learn to deal with temptation in God's wisdom and strength. Make no mistake, when you and I take God at His word and apply what He says to our lives, we experience the benefits of an undivided commitment to Christ. May you experience these benefits as you seek to live a life of integrity and deal with temptation in a God-honoring way.

spiritual integrity

Surviving the Storms

Key Verse

Consider it all joy, my brethren, when you encounter various trials, knowing that the testing of your faith produces endurance. And let endurance have its perfect result, so that you may be perfect and complete, lacking in nothing. (James 1:2-4, NASB)

Goals for Growth

- Recognize that God allows trials in our lives to build our character.
- Understand how to stand strong in trials.
- Commit to praying instead of complaining.

Head Start

Show us a man who survives the trials of life, and we'll show you a man of great character. The fact is, character grows strong during times of trial, especially when we choose to hang tough. No man likes trials. We endure them because we have to, not because we want to. We are tempted to fold or to try to escape the hard times. It's easy to give in and grow bitter, but it's character-building when we choose to weather the storms of life through perseverance and prayer.

Who enjoys coming home after a busy day at work to a pile of unpaid bills, an exhausted wife, wound-up kids, and doggy-do duty? Let's go deeper. How do we handle a job layoff? How about an unexpected illness or your wife's abrupt departure from your marriage?

The apostle James tells us to rejoice amidst such situations, to endure them for our good. But how could we possibly be joyful about the hardships we face? What good could possibly come out of openly welcoming these situations in our lives? Surely James is in the minority on this one! If I (Todd) had written the book of James, it would start like this:

Trials stink. Nobody likes them. So get on with life and get out of the situation that is causing you so much grief. Is it a boss? Then find a new job. Is it an employee? Then downsize. Is it a spouse? Then hasta la bye-bye, baby. Is it financial hardship? Then refinance and bet on lucky sevens. Just get out and get on with your life! Life is too short to be hassling with a load of crud.

(Aren't you glad I didn't write the New Testament? I know God is. At times the way I think is so warped that people are amazed to discover that I'm a pastor with actual Bible degrees.)

Amazing though it may seem, James isn't telling us to find a way *out* of our trials, but rather to stay where we are and endure them. If you think James was off his rocker, consider what others in the Bible said about hardship:

It was good for me to be afflicted so that I might learn your decrees. (Psalm 119:71)

In this world you will have trouble. But take heart! I have overcome the world. (John 16:33)

For our light and momentary troubles are achieving for us an eternal glory that far outweighs them all. (2 Corinthians 4:17)

Dear friends, do not be surprised at the painful trial you are suffering, as though something strange were happening to you. (1 Peter 4:12)

I'm not making this stuff up. The Bible is clear: Your hardships are the Lord's instruments in your life to make you into a man of God. I honestly wish there were another way, but there isn't. In fact, it is never God's will for you to run from your problems—except when it comes to sexual temptation. (In that case, God wants you to turn on your heels and run like crazy!)

Connect with the Word

Read James 1:1-12.

1. What kinds of trials do you think James is referring to in this passage? Why do you think he exhorts us to respond with a joyful heart during times of trial or testing?

2. What do you think a joyful heart looks like in the midst of a trial?

3. How does tested faith produce endurance?

4. Why do we fail the test when we respond to life's trials with a bad attitude, a complaining spirit, or an attempt to run from the situation?

5. The word *endure* means "to stand under." What makes it possible to stand under—or endure—a trial? Think of a trial you faced in the past or are facing now. Describe what helped (or is helping) you stand under it in a godly way.

6. According to verse 4, what is the purpose of enduring a trial to the end with a joyful heart?

7. What kind of prayer can you pray in the midst of a trial (verse 5)?

8. In verses 9-11, James contrasts humility (poverty) with pride (riches). How does remaining humble in the midst of a trial help you discover God's purpose for you in that trial?

Connect with the Group

Group Opener

Read the group opener aloud and discuss the questions that follow. (Suggestion: As you begin your group discussion time in each of the following sessions, consider forming smaller groups of three to six men. This will allow more time for discussion and give everyone an opportunity to share their thoughts and struggles.)

When Frank Brinner married his sweetheart, Patsy, he didn't have a clue that life would turn out the way it has. Early in their marriage, he enjoyed a successful company, two athletic sons, and a vibrant faith in Christ. Who could ask for more?

Yet two years into their marriage, the Brinners received the most devastating news of their lives. Patsy was diagnosed with multiple sclerosis, and it would change their lives forever. That was over twenty years ago. Ever since then, Frank has cared for his wife's needs on a daily basis. As her health has deteriorated, his care for her has become even more painstaking and emotionally draining.

Recently Frank talked with an old friend about a conversation he'd had with his wife. Jokingly Frank had told Patsy, "Honey, I've taken such good care of you that I have all the gray hair. You have none." They laughed together.

That exchange illustrates the upbeat, loving, sacrificial, and joy-filled attitude that has marked the past two decades of Frank's life. Refusing to grow bitter and miserable, he has chosen to deal with this trial joyfully. No man would ask for a trial like that. But such challenges come our way whether we like it or not. We don't get to choose our trials, but we do get to choose our responses to them.

Discussion Questions

a. In what ways can you relate to a trial like Frank's? How do you typically respond when you are faced with a daunting challenge?

b. What are some of the harmful ways men tend to respond to trials?

c. What's the difference between *enduring* a trial and *experiencing joy* in a trial? How does joy enable us to endure a trial?

d. What do you think is the basis of joy?

e. According to verses 2-4, what bottom-line benefits do we experience when we rejoice in our trials?

f. What do you think James expects us to do in order to stand under a trial that seems overwhelming?

g. During times of testing, how is "double-mindedness" revealed in our prayers?

h. In verses 9-12, James described being rich materially but poor spiritually. How do trials tend to reverse this condition in a man's life?

i. What kinds of trials are the men in your group experiencing these days? What can you do to help one another? How can you pray for one another?

Standing Strong

Identify the trials in your life that are threatening to sink your faith.

What can the guys in your group do this week to help you through one of your trials?

mental integrity

It All Starts in the Mind

Key Verse

But each one is tempted when he is carried away and enticed by his own lust. (James 1:14, NASB)

Goals for Growth

- Understand the origin of temptation.
- Realize that God isn't the one who tempts you.
- Commit to controlling your thought life before it controls you.

Head Start

Thoughts flood my mind every day. What I do with them determines who I become.

Do you believe that? Consider extramarital affairs, for example. They don't happen overnight. (Ask any man who's been through one.) They brew in a man's mind for weeks and months, even years. When our thoughts linger on a person or object for any length of time, desire naturally follows. If we long for God, that's good. But if we lust after sex, it's deadly.

In this week's passage, James identifies lust (*epithuma* in the Greek) as a temptation every man faces. *Epithuma* is a craving or longing, but it's much more than that; it's a sexual lust that bores deep into our hearts and tears up our character. True, there are different kinds of lusts. We crave money. We long for material possessions. We ache for acceptance. But there is nothing quite as powerful as sexual lust.

Most of us would like to eliminate sexual temptation from our lives. I'm sure you've thought many times, *If I just weren't tempted that way, I'd have this Christian thing whipped.* But the fact is, sexual temptation is a daily reality we must learn to deal with if we want to live godly lives.

In our ministry we (Todd and Kenny) counsel men who are battling lust in the workplace, checking out pornography on the Internet, and frequenting strip bars or adult clubs. As Steve Arterburn says in his introduction to *Every Man's Battle,*

> You're in a tough position. You live in a world awash with sensual images available twenty-four hours a day in a variety of mediums: print, television, videos, the Internet—even phones. But God offers you freedom from the slavery of sin through

the cross of Christ, and He created your eyes and mind with an ability to be trained and controlled. We simply have to stand up and walk by His power in the right path.[1]

Unfortunately, sexual temptation is a constant threat to our well-being. It's like a dangerously sharp rock submerged beneath the surface of the water that can potentially rip a huge gash in our hull and cause us to sink to the bottom. The frightening thing is that many of the men we counsel believe they'll be okay without confronting the problem directly. "It's not that bad," they say. "It's just a little mental compromise."

Satan sells us the lie that we can handle it. But where is God in all this? He's not the author of sin and sexual temptation; He's the Giver of good gifts. God's man must learn to resist temptation, run from it, and then replace it with God's better plan for his life. When we say no to temptation, it's critical that we follow with a yes to God and His way.

In this session you will learn that sexual temptation always starts with a thought. The mind is a very powerful thing. What you think about is important. As someone once put it, "Sow a thought, reap an action. Sow an action, reap a habit. Sow a habit, reap a character. Sow a character, reap a destiny."

---

1. Stephen Arterburn and Fred Stoeker, *Every Man's Battle* (Colorado Springs: WaterBrook Press, 2000), 4.

Connect with the Word

Read James 1:13-14.

1. Have you ever blamed God for your struggles with temptation? Why or why not?

2. If God is not the author of temptation, then how does He use it in our lives? (See Job 1:12; Matthew 6:13; 1 Corinthians 10:13.)

3. How does lust carry us away and entice us? What is your experience with this?

4. How have your thoughts contributed to sexual sin in the past?

Read 2 Samuel 11:1-15.

5. What kind of havoc did a stray thought cause King David?

6. Where did this spiral into sin begin for him?

7. What should David have done between verses 2 and 3 that he didn't do?

Connect with the Group

Group Opener
Read the group opener aloud and discuss the questions that follow.

It all started with an innocent conversation at work. Who knew that Chris would end up in a yearlong affair with a woman he thought was just an acquaintance? On a business trip to Las Vegas, she and Chris danced and then kissed. It doesn't take much.

What started as an innocent conversation ended in a string of lies, sexual liaisons, and more pain and hurt than God ever intended for a married couple to endure. Satan wants us to believe that this is all innocent stuff, that we can flirt with, get emotionally attached to, and even touch someone other than our spouse and still not violate our marriage covenant.

Wrong.

Thankfully for Chris, after years of brokenness, counseling, forgiveness, and the rebuilding of trust, his marriage and family have been restored. He never wants to experience that pain again. He once told me, "Todd, it was like having to start all over again. I had to go back to square one. The pleasure wasn't worth all the pain."

Consider the truth revealed by Stephen Arterburn and Fred Stoeker in *Every Man's Battle:*

For males, impurity of the eyes is sexual foreplay.

That's right. Just like stroking an inner thigh or rubbing a breast. Because foreplay is any sexual action that naturally takes us down the road to intercourse. Foreplay ignites passions, rocketing us by stages until we go all the way....

If you're married, you may be asking, What does all this have to do with me? My foreplay happens only with my wife.

Are you sure? Impurity of the eyes provides definite sexual gratification. Isn't *that* foreplay? When you see a hot movie scene, is there a twitch below your belt? What are you thinking when you're on the beach and suddenly meet a jaw-dropping beauty in a thong bikini? You gasp while Mission Control drones, "We have ignition!" You have her in bed on the spot,

though only in your mind. Or you file away the image and
fantasize about her later.[2]

Discussion Questions

a. If you had been Chris's best friend, how would you have coun-
seled him at each stage of his fall into sin?

b. Do you agree with Chris's final assessment of his experience, that
the pleasure isn't worth all the pain? Why or why not?

c. Have you ever considered the idea of *visual foreplay?* How do
you react to this concept? Explain.

---

2. Arterburn and Stoeker, *Every Man's Battle,* 66-7.

d. Is it a sin to be tempted? Why or why not? Do we ever bring temptation on ourselves? (See Proverbs 7:6-23 and Hebrews 4:15.) Explain.

e. What arguments or excuses do we tend to use to rationalize our wrong responses to sexual temptation?

f. When are men most vulnerable to sexual sin?

g. What steps can we take to deal effectively with lust before it becomes sin?

h. According to the following verses, what can we do to control our thoughts?

Psalm 119:9-11

Proverbs 4:23

2 Corinthians 10:5

Philippians 4:6-8

i. What can we do this week as a group to help one another in our struggles with sexual temptation and sin?

Standing Strong

Read Ephesians 5:11-13, then list your biggest areas of sexual temptation. (Remember: The more specific you are in your response, the more helpful this exercise will be to you.)

Complete the statement below, reflecting the kind of man you believe God wants you to be.

As a result of this week's study on sexual integrity and the mind, with God's help, I will:

Use the following phrase to memorize the six virtues from Philippians 4:8 (NASB) that we are to think about: "Thoughts have a righteous purpose. Love, God."

Thoughts = *True*
Have = *Honorable*
Righteous = *Right*
Purpose = *Pure*
Love = *Lovely*
God = *Good Repute*

Put the following principles into practice this week:
- Watch what you feed your mind.
- Win the battle each moment by turning your thoughts toward God.

sexual integrity

The Other Woman

Key Verse

Then when lust has conceived, it gives birth to sin; and when sin is accomplished, it brings forth death. (James 1:15, NASB)

Goals for Growth

- Understand that wrongful actions lead to sin's entanglements.
- Become fully aware of the consequences of giving in to temptation.
- Acknowledge and accept God's help to stand strong.

Head Start

It's one thing to encounter a lustful thought; it's another to act on it. You know the difference. You are sitting in church, and as you look at a woman nearby, the thought crosses your mind, *That woman has more than a nice outfit on.* What we do with our thoughts at times like these will either lead us to victory over sin or increase our vulnerability to it. Sure, you may not act upon your thought at that very moment, but if you dwell on it—and keep coming back to it—you will become increasingly vulnerable to sin.

Someone once said, "Be careful what you think about. Your thoughts could become actions at any moment." Those are wise words. Let me say it again: It's one thing to be tempted with a lustful thought. It's another to act on it. What's the difference? If a fantasy is allowed to camp out in your mind, you've already given in. And James said it will lead to sin.

Most men don't fully realize the connection between thoughts and actions until it is too late. One look leads to another. One thought leads to another. We start to graze with our eyes, and no one has a clue. We can feast all day long with our eyes and our minds, and no one seems to get hurt. But eventually, James said, this lust conceives and gives birth to a tangible sinful action.

The majority of men who are caught in sexual addiction did not plan to go that far. They will tell you it all started with a crazy idea. That's enough to scare every one of us into doing a better job of paying attention to what we think about. Or, to use even more graphic language: James's strong words should be enough to clobber us into shape!

Connect with the Word

Read James 1:15-18.

1. According to the word picture James used in verse 15, how is lust similar to pregnancy?

2. Does sexual sin always result in death? (See Proverbs 7:21-23.) What kind of death?

3. In what ways are you being deceived by sexual sin these days?

4. God doesn't leave you empty-handed in your struggle against lust. What help does He offer you (verses 17 and 18)?

5. James describes our worth to God in verse 18. How does our sense of worth help us avoid giving in to sexual sin?

Read Genesis 39:1-9.

6. What did Joseph do to "deserve" this temptation? Do you think he brought this on himself? Why or why not? Are we ever at fault when we're tempted? (See Proverbs 7:6-23.) Explain.

7. Joseph was tempted to have sex with Potiphar's wife. How did he respond to her advances?

8. What is the cost of giving in to temptation? What is the benefit of resisting? (See Proverbs 6:26-28; 5:15-19.)

Connect with the Group

Group Opener
Read the group opener aloud and discuss the questions that follow.

Sexual impurity has become rampant in the church because we've ignored the costly work of obedience to God's standards as individuals, asking too often, "How far can I go and still be called a Christian?" We've crafted an image and may even *seem* sexually pure while permitting our eyes to play freely when no one is around, avoiding the hard work of *being* sexually pure.[3]

God is waiting for you. But He is not waiting by the altar, hoping you'll drop by and talk for a while. He is waiting for you to rise up and engage in the battle. We have power through the Lord to overcome every level of sexual immorality, but if we don't utilize that power, we'll never break free of the habit.[4]

Discussion Questions

a. Discuss your reactions to the two quotes above. What do you agree or disagree with? What would you say differently? What personal experience, if any, confirms something either quote conveys?

---

3. Arterburn and Stoeker, *Every Man's Battle,* 58.
4. Arterburn and Stoeker, *Every Man's Battle,* 92.

b. How do we get trapped in sexual sin? What lies do we tell ourselves that intensify our struggle? What can we do to break free?

c. What role can another man play in helping you win the war
   against sexual sin? How can we make this work within our own
   small group?

d. What did you learn from your study of Joseph that will help you
   avoid sexual sin in the future?

Standing Strong

Last week you identified the biggest areas of sexual temptation in your life. This week consider the following: What three ways are you being tempted to *act* on sexual temptation? What can the men in your group do to help you stand strong?

Complete the statement below, reflecting the man you believe God wants you to be.

As a result of this week's study on sexual integrity and actions, with God's help, I will:

This week, start building into your life three perimeters of defense against sexual temptation:
1. your eyes—refuse to look at things you know will tempt you
2. your mind—screen your thoughts
3. your heart—commit to Christ daily

biblical integrity

In One Ear and Out the Other?

Key Verse

Prove yourselves doers of the word, and not merely hearers who delude themselves. (James 1:22, NASB)

Goals for Growth

- Realize that selective obedience is not God's will.
- Identify areas of selective obedience in your own life.
- Experience the freedom and joy of complete loyalty to God's Word.

Head Start

We men can talk a good line. We love to fudge a little with the truth. We have the most amazing ability to project an image of ourselves that is something other than reality. We *say* we have it together…but does it really come together on the playing field of life?

I know a guy who was a self-described captain of the USC football team. Was he really? Did that accurately reflect the truth? Technically speaking it was true because school tradition allowed all graduating seniors to be "captain" for the final game of the season. But he was "captain" for only one game, and he had to share this honor with dozens of other seniors!

Similarly, it's easy to *say* you are a Christian, but do you *live* like one? It's easy to fudge when it comes to obeying the Word of God. In Matthew 7:24 Jesus said, "Everyone who hears these words of mine and puts them into practice is like a wise man who built his house on the rock." Does this describe you? When God says in His Word to do something, do you do it? Or do you withhold full obedience to God in certain areas of your life?

Our flesh and pride love "allowable" deviations, shades of gray, and acts of compromise. All of these diminish God's authority in our lives and increase our own. But James points out that we cannot mix our own standards with God's. When we do, we lose our biblical integrity.

When you know God's standard but rationalize not following it, the only person you are fooling is yourself. We often fool ourselves into thinking that we're doing pretty well when it comes to acting on what the Bible commands us to do. But if we're honest, we have to admit that we fall short of wholeheartedly living out what God asks of us. We read His Word, but all too often His commands go in one ear and out the other.

Do you obey God in every area of your life? This is the ultimate test for biblical integrity. Let's look at what the book of James has to say about it.

Connect with the Word

Read James 1:21-27.

1. According to verse 21, what gets in the way of our obedience? Why are these footholds for sin in our lives?

2. What can you do to maintain a humble attitude when receiving instruction from the Lord?

3. What are some of the practical differences between doers of the Word and hearers of the Word?

4. Describe the man in verse 25. What does he do? What are the benefits of these actions? In what ways are you like or unlike this man?

5. What are the proofs of obedience described in verses 26 and 27? What steps can you take to become more obedient in these areas?

Connect with the Group

Group Opener
Read the group opener aloud and discuss the questions that follow.

Why would a California family go to Chicago in March? Well, we all (Todd's family) wanted to see the last snowfall while visiting some good friends. We had to catch a flight home through Denver, and on our way to the gate, I was not impressed with our progress. I was worried that we'd miss our connection unless someone in our party picked up the pace. So I barked out some orders to my wife to "get moving."

Let's just say I failed to accomplish my objective. My wife glared back at me and refused to speed up. When we arrived at the gate in plenty of time to make the flight, I realized immediately that I had a choice to make. Would I rationalize away my sin, or would I admit my wrongdoing and ask for forgiveness?

I decided to take the high road and obey what the Word says. I apologized in front of the kids and half the passengers waiting to board. I'm glad to report that my wife was also obedient in forgiving me.

Often, obedience is the difference between *knowing* the right thing to do and *doing* it. And sometimes it will cost you more than a little pride.

Discussion Questions

a. What would you have done in Todd's place?

b. What are the most common ways we selectively obey God's Word?

c. *Partial obedience is better than no obedience at all.* Do you agree with this statement? Why or why not? How do you think James would respond?

d. In what ways do we partially obey these days? Give some practical examples.

e. Why do we tend to *hear* the Word more than *do* the Word?

f. Which areas of obedience mentioned in verses 26 and 27 are you currently struggling with?

g. According to verse 26, what is a "worthless" religion? How can we, as a group, avoid that kind of religion in the future?

Standing Strong
In what area(s) of your life is God asking you to be more fully obedient?

List the ways you are taking shortcuts or are practicing selective obedience.

Complete the statement below, reflecting the man you believe God wants you to be.

As a result of this week's study on biblical integrity, with God's help, I will:

behavioral integrity

Judging by Appearances

Key Verse

The LORD said to Samuel, "Do not consider his appearance or his height, for I have rejected him. The LORD does not look at the things man looks at. Man looks at the outward appearance, but the LORD looks at the heart." (1 Samuel 16:7)

Goals for Growth

- Learn to treat people fairly.
- Grow more sensitive to all people, regardless of their professional status.
- Realize that wealth does not make the man.

Head Start

When my wife and I (Todd) go out to dinner, I often self-park. (All right, I *always* self-park.) As we approach the front of the restaurant, it's hard not to notice the $85,000 dark blue Jag, the bright red Porsche, and the silver BMW strategically parked halfway into the restaurant.

I bet you've never thought, *So who's the big shot who gets to park in front? I wish I had friends like that!* or *I wish I had money like that!* Oh, the dagger penetrates deep into the flesh...

Comparison is a natural tendency for men. We like to measure a man by his possessions and status. It makes us feel good to find someone lower on the ladder. However, the Bible teaches that net worth does not equal self-worth. Ask James. When we put others down or judge them on the basis of their appearance, status, income, or talent, we become poor judges of character. Comparison spoils our relationships and robs us of the joy of seeing the true worth of others. It also points out our own insecurities and judgmental attitudes.

Yet it's so tempting to compare, especially in the workplace! We compare ourselves professionally and financially with other men. When we meet another man, the first question we ask is, "What do you do for a living?" We immediately begin sizing him up. *What kind of car does he drive? What kind of clothes does he wear? Where does he live?* We size up others in the workplace based upon position and income. As a result, we play political games and aren't authentic in our relationships. We don't treat others as we'd like to be treated.

Instead, we treat them based on their worth to us, not on their worth to God.

Sadly, James said the same problem exists in the church. Even there we tend to measure others according to the wrong standards. Yet the Bible redefines *rich*. The truly rich man does not show favoritism; rather, he keeps the "royal law": "Love your neighbor as yourself" (James 2:8).

Connect with the Word

Read James 2:1-13.

1. Why did James say in verse 4 that making comparisons is the same as becoming "judges with evil motives" (NASB)?

2. When are you most tempted to compare yourself with others and judge them? How do you handle this temptation?

3. What does James say in verses 5-7 about the poor and the rich? In light of this passage, what is the right way to view others?

4. Why did James bring the royal law into the picture in verse 8? (See also Matthew 22:34-40.)

5. According to verse 8, which one of the laws sets you free from making comparisons? Why do you think this works? How do you envision it working in real life?

6. What is the appropriate way to treat others? When do you need to be especially committed to obedience in this area?

Read 1 Samuel 16:1-13.

7. Why did Samuel try to select the next king based on appearance? What did God say to correct him?

Connect with the Group

Group Opener

When have you totally misjudged someone based on appearance alone?
When have you been misjudged based on appearance?

Discussion Questions

a. What harm is there in comparing yourself with others? in judging others? What do these actions say about the kind of person you are?

b. Read Ephesians 6:9. How does this verse reinforce the point that we sometimes treat others wrongly?

c. Looks often deceive. In what ways does James help us avoid judging others based on appearance?

d. How do you want others to see you?

e. What did James mean when he spoke of fulfilling the royal law completely?

f. According to Romans 12:9-20, how are we to treat others?

g. What can we do to be more merciful in our relationships? Give some practical examples.

Standing Strong

List some ways in which you are being judgmental or are showing partiality in your workplace or in other settings.

What steps are you going take this week to avoid being judgmental?

Complete the statement below, reflecting the man you believe God wants you to be.

As a result of this week's study on behavioral integrity, with God's help, I will:

verbal integrity

Loose Lips

Key Verse

We all stumble in many ways. If anyone is never at fault in what he says, he is a perfect man, able to keep his whole body in check. (James 3:2)

Goals for Growth

- Learn to think before you speak.
- Understand the power of your words.
- Speak words that build up rather than tear down.

Head Start

Be honest. You said something you didn't mean to say. You wish you could take the words back, but you can't. The worst part is that the person who heard you say them won't forget them. Been there?

Did you know that the tongue is the fastest healing body part? Unfortunately, the damage the tongue causes is slow to heal and can last a lifetime. Words are like toothpaste. Once they come out, they can't be stuffed back in. The tongue gets us into trouble more often than any other part of our anatomy. It's just too easy to speak without thinking.

The Bible teaches that we're either using our words to build others up or to tear them down. The temptation is to lift ourselves up by tearing others down. It's the tyranny of the tongue. It lights fires we can't extinguish.

Kenny and I (Todd) have a friend, Jeff, who is a captain with the fire department. He tells the best stories. Jeff would be the first to tell you how difficult it is to extinguish a fire once it has been started. Dry brush fires in the middle of the summer are the worst. "It ain't going out anytime soon," he'll say.

But what fires have you set ablaze with your tongue this week? Fires in your marriage? with your kids? at the office? with a slow grocery attendant? with that rude driver in the silver Gremlin on the freeway?

Jesus said, "Out of the overflow of the heart the mouth speaks" (Matthew 12:34). The tongue is an indicator, revealing to us the depth of our character. The question is, What can we do to transform the heart that is reflected in our speech? Let's explore what James has to say.

Connect with the Word

Read James 3.

1. According to verses 2 and 3, how does the tongue control the whole body?

2. What did James say about the rudder of a ship? How does this illustration apply to the tongue (verse 4)?

3. In what way is an improper word or statement like a lit match in a brittle and dry forest?

4. What are some practical steps you could take to tame your own tongue this week?

5. What can you learn about the tongue from the following proverbs? Write one truth you learn from each passage.

Proverbs 10:19

Proverbs 12:25

Proverbs 15:18

Proverbs 16:24

Proverbs 17:27-28

Proverbs 25:11

Proverbs 25:28

Matthew 12:34

Matthew 15:11-20

6. Either we curse or we bless. What are some ways you can bless another person with your tongue?

7. Look at James 1:19-20. Why do you think angry words get in the way of God's desire to produce righteousness in us?

Connect with the Group

Group Opener
Read the group opener aloud and discuss the questions that follow.

My (Todd's) daughter, Brooke, is an excellent soccer player. Since she doesn't have the height of the other team members, she has to compensate on the playing field with speed and aggressive play.

During one of her games, she was told to guard Number 8—the opponents' "scoring machine"—with her life. The coach yelled, "Brooke, stay on her. Wherever she goes, you go. Whatever you do, don't let her score."

Brooke went for it and rubbed shoulders with this girl every time she got the ball. After the game she told me that Number 8 yelled at her, repeatedly saying, "If you touch me again, I'm going to push you to the ground."

Brooke responded, "I'm not here to trade insults. I'm here to play soccer."

I can't tell you how proud that made me feel. Who taught her to say that? Probably her mother, because I would have gone for the jugular. Even though she wanted to return fire, she held her tongue. After the game, Number 8 apologized to Brooke for her threats and mean words.

When *you're* ambushed, how do you respond? Do you respond in anger? Or, like Brooke, do you consider your response first and then speak?

Discussion Questions

a. We've all said things we later regretted. Tell the group about an experience you've had when you lost control of your tongue. What happened?

b. In what situations are you most likely to "let it rip" these days?

c. Which word picture about the tongue in James 3:1-12 had the strongest impact on you? Explain.

d. What did you learn from your study of the passages in Proverbs and Matthew?

e. What can we do to clean up our speech and speak only blessings instead of curses? (See Proverbs 18:21.)

f. What relationship(s) in your life will benefit most from your tamed tongue?

g. Ultimately, God is the tamer of tongues. What is your part? What is His part?

Standing Strong

Who, if anyone, do you need to apologize to for words you spoke in anger? Who, if anyone, can you call this week and build up in Christ's love? Share the results with your group during the next session.

Using the following chart, take an inventory of your words. Commit to speaking words this week that will build others up rather than destroy.

Words That DESTROY	*Words That BUILD UP*

moral integrity

The Gods of This World

Key Verse

He gives us more grace. That is why Scripture says: "God opposes the proud but gives grace to the humble." (James 4:6)

Goals for Growth

- Identify worldly tendencies in your life.
- Understand the destructive nature of materialism.
- Learn the remedy for a pride-filled life marked by worldliness.

Head Start

We love toys, don't we? I (Todd) have an awesome mountain bike that my family and friends gave me when I turned forty. It has full suspension and can climb almost vertical inclines. (Okay, that last part is an exaggeration. The bike may be able to handle verticals, but I can't.) The point is, it's a really great bike.

But—believe it or not—even though I have such a great bike, I want another one. So, why am I not satisfied with the one I have? Here's the thing: Kenny went bike shopping after I got mine, and he one-upped me. You see, I got the Trek Fuel 90; Kenny bought the Trek Fuel 98, which is just a little lighter, a little stronger, a little more versatile—and a *little* more expensive. When does this bike envy ever end?

I can't stand that Kenny's bike is better than mine. Every time we ride, I think, *I should have gotten the Fuel 98! What was I thinking? What's with my lousy family and friends? Didn't they know? Don't they care?* The sad thing is, at that point, I'm all torn up inside over a bike. Maybe I'll just have to buy a Trek Fuel 100, like our friend Paul just got...

The apostle James would say to us, "More is *not* better. And more often than not, more will get you into trouble." In James 4:1 he wrote, "Pleasures...wage war in your members" (NASB), and "Desires...battle within you." The fact is, the battle really is inside us. What you crave sets you up for a battle with yourself, with others, and with God. James said that God resists people like that.

Sadly, for most of us, the taste of the good life has created an unquenchable appetite. It drives the average man to work harder than God intended. Worse, it creates an ever-increasing hunger for things. We want what we don't need, and we fight to get it in order to impress those we don't even know. We become sidetracked with worthless pursuits. If you live in the United States, you are probably battling materialism and the greener-grass syndrome, regardless of which side of the tracks you live on.

What's the problem with desiring more? James compared worldliness to committing adultery against God. When we befriend the world, we are committing spiritual adultery! We are being unfaithful to God! It's that serious. Just like a wife who knows when her husband is being overly friendly with another woman, God's Spirit is grieved when our heart's affections turn away from Him toward pleasures, possessions, and power. We need to end the affair—ASAP.

Connect with the Word

Read James 4:1-10,13-17.

1. What kind of desires was James referring to in verse 1?

2. How do our desires get us into trouble?

3. According to this passage, what does friendship with the world look like? What does it look like in your own life?

4. What practical antidote to worldliness do you find in verses 7-10?

5. In verses 13-17, what kind of man was James describing? According to James, what's wrong with this man's thinking? What should he be thinking?

6. How can our determination to be successful lead us down a false path? When have you experienced this in your own life?

Connect with the Group

Group Opener
Read the group opener aloud and discuss the questions that follow.

Jack is not a man of means, but he feels compelled to live like a man of means. His circumstances call for financial discipline, but his lifestyle has given him an image to keep up. He leases an expensive sports car, shops at the most expensive stores, and provides his wife with any earthly comfort he or she can imagine they "need." Jack's circumstances say *X* but he is spending like *Y.* His image and his reality simply do not jibe. He is driven to maintain the appearance at all costs—and that can only mean that the world has got him. He's living in a house of (credit) cards that's destined to collapse at any moment. As the mountain of debt reaches greater heights, his faith suffers and his marriage is going down the toilet.

For what? For the image the world has told him he needs to live up to.[5]

Discussion Questions

a. If you were Jack's best friend, what would you say to him about his obsession with image and material possessions? What first step would you recommend he take toward breaking free?

b. In general, what are the signs of materialism in a man's life? What are the signs in your own life?

---

5. Stephen Arterburn and Kenny Luck, *Every Man, God's Man* (Colorado Springs: WaterBrook Press, 2003), 76.

c. Define worldly pleasures in light of this week's Scripture passage.

d. In what ways have you formed a friendship with the world?

e. What steps does James tell us to take in order to overcome worldliness and materialism? Is this easy or difficult for you? Explain.

f. The businessman who says in verse 13, "We will go...and make a profit" (NASB) is oblivious to the fact that life is uncertain. Why is the businessman's way of thinking wrong? Describe a time, if any, when you had a similar outlook on life.

g. In what ways does a materialistic focus impact our relationships? Share a personal example, if you can.

Standing Strong

Of these three—power, possessions, and pleasure—which tempts you the most at the moment? List specific issues you face in that area:

Complete the statement below, reflecting the man you believe God wants you to be.

As a result of this week's study on moral integrity, with God's help, I will:

relational integrity

Friendly but Friendless?

Key Verse

Confess your sins to each other and pray for each other so that you may be healed. The prayer of a righteous man is powerful and effective. (James 5:16)

Goals for Growth

- Identify the barriers to male accountability.
- Be willing to become accountable to other men.
- Learn to confess your sins to another man.

Head Start

Consider the proverbial friendless American male who lives in isolation from others. It's more common than you think. I'm continually amazed that we can physically stand a few inches from another man's face, yet be hundreds of miles away emotionally.

Can you relate? We all live in our own secret worlds, thinking we can work out our own problems. Why do we do this? It's simple. We fear exposure. For years we have projected an image that we have it all together, that we're just fine. So when sin creeps in, instead of getting another man's help, we cover up our pain and failure. We go stealth.

Have you let anyone into your secret world and allowed the lies you have been living to be exposed? Do you have a friend who *really* knows you? You may say, "I don't need another man; I have my wife." Men, God did not create your wife to be your accountability partner. You have to have a male friend. Men become men in the company of men, not women. James said that there will come a time when you are either suffering, sick, or in sin. Who will be there for you when that happens?

So I ask the question again: *Who in your life notices when you are living on the edge of sin?* Who notices when things are not right with you—and then asks you about it? Can you name a friend who is invaluable to your spiritual well-being?

Let's face it, we're going to mess up. The question is, Who's going to bring us back from the edge?

Connect with the Word

Read James 5:13-20.

1. Why is it the responsibility of the one who is sick or suffering to call the elders to pray for him? What is James trying to get us to do?

2. How does praying with another person help us through our problems? When have you benefited from this?

3. How does unconfessed sin create roadblocks to spiritual growth? Where do you see such blockages in your life?

4. Why do you think we should confess our sins to one another? What good will it do? (See Ephesians 5:11-13.) Have you ever done this with another man? Explain. According to verses 16 and 17, what are the benefits of confessing our sins to one another?

5. What will God do through you when you take accountability seriously (verses 15, 16, 19, and 20)?

6. Why do you think James referred to Elijah in this passage? In what ways do you think Elijah as a man of God illustrates accountability?

7. How do we actually turn another person from sin?

Connect with the Group

Group Opener
Read the group opener aloud and discuss the questions that follow.

I (Todd) was hardly married five years before a good buddy came up to me and said, "Todd, either you go get help, or I'm going straight to your pastor with this." That got my attention. All right, then, the last thing I needed on my hands was full exposure of a problem that I'd been battling for five years.

My marriage! Gee thanks, Matt, ole buddy, friend, traitor, tattle-tale, bonehead. So I took the initiative and went to marriage counseling with my wife. I never realized how much trouble I was in until I sat in the counselor's office and he said, "Okay, let's begin."

"Where?" I asked.

"Let's start where it hurts."

My wife and I began bawling like babies.

As I look back I realize I might never have gotten there and done the hard work of shoring up my marriage if it hadn't been for my buddy Matt. He saved me from a firestorm. My wife was just hanging on, and I didn't even know it. I'd clearly neglected her emotionally while I was busy going to seminary. The irony of that kills me to this day. How could I have let that happen?

Thanks, Matt. I owe you one.

Discussion Questions

a. Describe a time when you were saved from a relational firestorm.

b. What are the reasons men don't open up with one another about their current or potential firestorms?

c. What are the consequences of leading both an unconfessed and a secretive life? (See Proverbs 28:13.)

d. In what ways does isolation breed sickness? Does God expect us to heal in isolation? Do you see any connection between sickness and sin in James 5:13-20? Explain. (Pastor Rick Warren says that "You are as sick as your secrets." And Steve Arterburn says, "Openness is to healing what secrets are to sickness.")

e. What would life look like if God's men practiced biblical confession? What effect can our prayers have on others who are in trouble?

f. When is it right to "go after" another man caught in sin? (See Galatians 6:1-5.)

g. Who in your life could you trust with your darkest secrets? Are you willing to ask this friend to hold you accountable? Why or why not?

Standing Strong

If you knew you wouldn't be shamed or embarrassed, what is one struggle you would want another man to know about?

In whom would you confide your struggle? Pray about it, then write his name below. Commit to talking with him about your struggle the next time you get together.

Complete the statement below, reflecting the man you believe God wants you to be.

As a result of this week's study on relational integrity, with God's help, I will:

small-group resources

What if men aren't doing the Connect with the Word section before our small-group session?

Don't be discouraged. You set the pace. If you are doing the study and regularly referring to it in conversations with your men throughout the week, they will pick up on its importance. Here are some suggestions to motivate the men in your group to do their home Bible study:

- Send out a midweek e-mail in which you share your answer to one of the study questions. This shows them that you are personally committed to and involved in the study.

- Ask the guys to hit "respond to all" on their e-mail program and share one insight from that week's Bible study with the entire group. Encourage them to send it out before the next small-group session.

- Every time you meet, ask each man in the group to share one insight from his home study.

What if men are not showing up for small group?

This might mean they are losing a sin battle and don't want to admit it to the group. Or they might be consumed with other priorities. Or maybe they don't think they're getting anything out of the group. Here are some suggestions for getting the guys back each week:

- Affirm them when they show up, and tell them how much it means to you that they make small group a priority.

- From time to time, ask them to share one reason they think small group is important to them.
- Regularly call or send out an e-mail the day before you meet to remind them you're looking forward to seeing them.
- Check in with any guy who has missed more than one session, and find out what's going on in his life.
- Get some feedback from the men. You may need to adjust your style. Listen and learn.

What if group discussion is not happening?

You are a discussion facilitator. You have to keep guys involved in the discussion or you'll lose them. You can engage a man who isn't sharing by saying, "Chuck, you've been quiet. What do you think about this question or discussion?" You should also be prepared to share your own personal stories that are related to the discussion questions. You'll set the example by the kind of sharing you do.

What if one man is dominating the group time?

You have to deal with it. If you don't, men will stop showing up. No one wants to hear from just one guy all the time. It will quickly kill morale. Meet with the guy in person and privately. Firmly but gently suggest that he allow others more time to talk. Be positive and encouraging, but truthful. You might say, "Bob, I notice how enthusiastic you are about the group and how you're always prepared to share your thoughts with the group. But there are some pretty quiet guys in the group too. Have you noticed? Would you be willing to help me get them involved in speaking up?"

How do I get the guys in my group more involved?

Give them something to do. Ask one guy to bring a snack. Invite another to lead the prayer time (ask in advance). Have one guy sub for you one week as the leader. (Meet with him beforehand to walk through the group program and the time allotments for each segment.) Encourage another guy to lead a subgroup.

What if guys are not being vulnerable during the Standing Strong or prayer times?

You model openness. You set the pace. Honesty breeds honesty. Vulnerability breeds vulnerability. Are you being vulnerable and honest about your own problems and struggles? (This doesn't mean that you have to spill your guts each week or reveal every secret of your life.) Remember, men want an honest, on-their-level leader who strives to walk with God. (Also, as the leader, you need an accountability partner, perhaps another group leader.)

What will we do at the first session?

We encourage you to open by discussing the **Small-Group Covenant** we've included in this resource section. Ask the men to commit to the study, and then discuss how long it will take your group to complete each session. (We suggest 75-90 minute sessions.) Men find it harder to come up with excuses for missing a group session if they have made a covenant to the other men right at the start.

Begin to identify ways certain men can play a more active role in small group. Give away responsibility. You won't feel as burdened, and your men will grow from the experience. Keep in mind that this process can take a few weeks. Challenge men to fulfill one of the group roles identified later in this resource section. If no one steps forward to fill a role, say to one of the men, "George, I've noticed that you are comfortable praying in a group. Would you lead us each week during that time?"

How can we keep the group connected after we finish a study?
Begin talking about starting another Bible study before you finish this eight-week study. (There are six studies to choose from in the Every Man Bible study series.) Consider having a social time at the conclusion of the study, and encourage the men to invite a friend. This will help create momentum and encourage growth as you launch into another study with your group. There are probably many men in your church or neighborhood who aren't in small groups but would like to be. Be the kind of group that includes others.

As your group grows, consider choosing an apprentice leader who can take half the group into another room for the **Connect with the Group** time. That subgroup can stay together for prayer, or you can reconvene as a large group during that time. You could also meet for discussion as a large group, and then break into subgroups for **Standing Strong** and **prayer**.

If your group doubles in size, it might be a perfect opportunity to release your apprentice leader with half the group to start another group. Allow men to pray about this and make a decision as a group. Typically, the relational complexities that come into play when a small group births a new group work themselves out. Allow guys to choose which group they'd like to be a part of. If guys are slow in choosing one group or another, ask them individually to select one of the groups. Take the lead in making this happen.

Look for opportunities for your group to serve in the church or community. Consider a local outreach project or a short-term missions trip. There are literally hundreds of practical ways you can serve the Lord in outreach. Check with your church leaders to learn the needs in your congregation or community. Create some interest by sending out scouts who will return with a report for the group. Serving keeps men from becoming self-focused and ingrown. When you serve as a group, you will grow as a group.

using this study in a large-group format

Many church leaders are looking for biblically based curriculum that can be used in a large-group setting, such as a Sunday-school class, or for small groups within an existing larger men's group. Each of the Every Man Bible studies can be adapted for this purpose. In addition, this curriculum can become a catalyst for churches wishing to launch men's small groups or to build a men's ministry in their church.

Getting Started

Begin by getting the word out to men in your church, inviting them to join you for a men's study based on one of the topics in the Every Man Bible study series. You can place a notice in your church bulletin, have the pastor announce it from the pulpit, or pursue some other means of attracting interest.

Orientation Week

Arrange your room with round tables and chairs. Put approximately six chairs at each table.

Start your class in prayer and introduce your topic with a short but motivational message from any of the scriptures used in the Bible study. Hand out the curriculum and challenge the men to do their homework before each class. During this first session give the men some discussion questions based upon an overview of the material and have them talk things through just within their small group around the table.

Just before you wrap things up, have each group select a table host or leader. You can do this by having everyone point at once to the person at their table they feel would best facilitate discussion for future meetings.

Ask those newly elected table leaders to stay after for a few minutes, and offer them an opportunity to be further trained as small-group leaders as they lead discussions throughout the course of the study.

Subsequent Weeks

Begin in prayer. Then give a short message (15-25 minutes) based upon the scripture used for that lesson. Pull out the most motivating topics or points and strive to make the discussion relevant to the life of an everyday man and his world. Then leave time for each table to work through the discussion questions listed in the curriculum. Be sure the discussion facilitators at each table close in prayer.

At the end of the eight sessions, you might want to challenge each "table group" to become a small group, inviting them to meet regularly with their new small-group leader and continue building the relationships they've begun.

prayer request record

Date:
Name:
Prayer Request:
Praise:

Date:
Name:
Prayer Request:
Praise:

Date:
Name:
Prayer Request:
Praise:

Date:
Name:
Prayer Request:
Praise:

Date:
Name:
Prayer Request:
Praise:

defining group roles

Group Leader: Leads the lesson and facilitates group discussion.

Apprentice Leader: Assists the leader as needed, which may include leading the lesson.

Refreshment Coordinator: Maintains a list of who will provide refreshments. Calls group members on the list to remind them to bring what they signed up for.

Prayer Warrior: Serves as the contact person for prayer between sessions. Establishes a list of those willing to pray for needs that arise. Maintains the prayer-chain list and activates the chain as needed by calling the first person on the list.

Social Chairman: Plans any desired social events during group sessions or at another scheduled time. Gathers members for planning committees as needed.

small-group roster

Name:
Address:
Phone: E-mail:

Name:
Address:
Phone: E-mail:

Name:
Address:
Phone: E-mail:

Name:
Address:
Phone: E-mail:

Name:
Address:
Phone: E-mail:

Name:
Address:
Phone: E-mail:

spiritual checkup

Your answers to the statements below will help you determine which areas you need to work on in order to grow spiritually. Mark the appropriate letter to the left of each statement. Then make a plan to take one step toward further growth in each area. Don't forget to pray for the Lord's wisdom before you begin. Be honest. Don't be overly critical or rationalize your weaknesses.

Y = Yes
S = Somewhat or Sometimes
N = No

My Spiritual Connection with Other Believers

___I am developing relationships with Christian friends.

___I have joined a small group.

___I am dealing with conflict in a biblical manner.

___I have become more loving and forgiving than I was a year ago.

___I am a loving and devoted husband and father.

My Spiritual Growth

___I have committed to daily Bible reading and prayer.

___I am journaling on a regular basis, recording my spiritual growth.

___I am growing spiritually by studying the Bible with others.

___I am honoring God in my finances and personal giving.

___I am filled with joy and gratitude for my life, even during trials.

___I respond to challenges with peace and faith instead of anxiety and anger.

___I avoid addictive behaviors (excessive drinking, overeating, watching too much TV, etc.).

Serving Christ and Others

___I am in the process of discovering my spiritual gifts and talents.

___I am involved in ministry in my church.

___I have taken on a role or responsibility in my small group.

___I am committed to helping someone else grow in his spiritual walk.

Sharing Christ with Others

___I care about and am praying for those around me who are unbelievers.

___I share my experience of coming to know Christ with others.

___I invite others to join me in this group or for weekend worship services.

___I am seeing others come to Christ and am praying for this to happen.

___I do what I can to show kindness to people who don't know Christ.

Surrendering My Life for Growth

___I attend church services weekly.

___I pray for others to know Christ, and I seek to fulfill the Great Commission.

___I regularly worship God through prayer, praise, and music, both at church and at home.

___I care for my body through exercise, nutrition, and rest.

___I am concerned about using my energy to serve God's purposes instead of my own.

My Identity in the Lord

___I see myself as a beloved son of God, one whom God loves regardless of my sin.

___I can come to God in all of my humanity and know that He accepts me completely. When I fail, I willingly run to God for forgiveness.

___I experience Jesus as an encouraging Friend and Lord each moment of the day.

___I have an abiding sense that God is on my side. I am aware of His gracious presence with me throughout the day.

___During moments of beauty, grace, and human connection, I lift up praise and thanks to God.

___I believe that using my talents to their fullest pleases the Lord.

___I experience God's love for me in powerful ways.

small-group covenant

As a committed group member, I agree to the following:*

- **Regular Attendance.** I will attend group sessions on time and let everyone know in advance if I can't make it.
- **Group Safety.** I will help create a safe, encouraging environment where men can share their thoughts and feelings without fear of embarrassment or rejection. I will not judge another guy or attempt to fix his problems.
- **Confidentiality.** I will always keep to myself everything that is shared in the group.
- **Acceptance.** I will respect different opinions or beliefs and let Scripture be the teacher.
- **Accountability.** I will make myself accountable to the other group members for the personal goals I share.
- **Friendliness.** I will look for those around me who might join the group and explore their faith with other men.
- **Ownership.** I will prayerfully consider taking on a specific role within the group as the opportunity arises.
- **Spiritual Growth.** I will commit to establishing a daily quiet time with God, which includes doing the homework for this study. I will share with the group the progress I make and the struggles I experience as I seek to grow spiritually.

Signed: _____ Date: _____

---

*   *Permission is given to photocopy and distribute this form to each man in your group. Review this covenant quarterly or as needed.*

about the authors

 STEPHEN ARTERBURN is coauthor of the best-selling Every Man series. He is also founder and chairman of New Life Clinics, host of the daily *New Life Live!* national radio program, and creator of the Women of Faith conferences. A nationally known speaker and licensed minister, Stephen has authored more than forty books. He lives with his family in Laguna Beach, California.

 KENNY LUCK is president and founder of Every Man Ministries and coauthor of *Every Man, God's Man* and its companion workbook. He is division leader for men's small groups and teaches a men's interactive Bible study at Saddleback Church in Lake Forest, California. He and his wife, Chrissy, have three children and reside in Rancho Santa Margarita, California.

 TODD WENDORFF is a graduate of U.C. Berkeley and holds a Th.M. from Talbot School of Theology. He serves as a pastor of men's ministries at Saddleback Church and is an adjunct professor at Biola University. He is an author of the Doing Life Together Bible study series. Todd and his wife, Denise, live with their three children in Trabuco Canyon, California.

every man's battle workshops

from New Life Ministries

ew Life Ministries receives hundreds of calls every month from Christian men who are struggling to stay pure in the midst of daily challenges to their sexual integrity and from pastors who are looking for guidance in how to keep fragile marriages from falling apart all around them.

As part of our commitment to equip individuals to win these battles, New Life Ministries has developed biblically based workshops directly geared to answer these needs. These workshops are held several times per year around the country.

- Our workshops **for men** are structured to equip men with the tools necessary to maintain sexual integrity and enjoy healthy, productive relationships.

- Our workshops **for church leaders** are targeted to help pastors and men's ministry leaders develop programs to help families being attacked by this destructive addiction.

Some comments from previous workshop attendees:

"An awesome, life-changing experience. Awesome teaching, teacher, content and program." —DAVE

"God has truly worked a great work in me since the EMB workshop. I am fully confident that with God's help, I will be restored in my ministry position. Thank you for your concern. I realize that this is a battle, but I now have the weapons of warfare as mentioned in Ephesians 6:10, and I am using them to gain victory!" —KEN

"It's great to have a workshop you can confidently recommend to anyone without hesitation, knowing that it is truly life changing. Your labors are not in vain!" —DR. BRAD STENBERG, Pasadena, CA

If sexual temptation is threatening your marriage or your church, please call **1-800-NEW-LIFE** to speak with one of our specialists.